A SEASON OF LOVE

 **HOWARD BOOKS**
A DIVISION OF SIMON & SCHUSTER
New York   London   Toronto   Sydney

MAL AUSTIN

picture · psalms   *an illustrated meditation*

INTRODUCTION

I CAN THINK OF NO BETTER FLOWER TO REPRESENT
LOVE THAN THE ROSE.

All the images in this book come from the 201 roses that
are found in my own garden. No plant seems to be as reliant
upon human time, effort, and attention. As with the love in
any relationship, good gardeners don't just have a few roses
growing in a plot of ground, they have a working relationship
with the roses. They study and learn what each rose requires
and come to realize the roses are dependent on the gardener
to give and then selflessly give more as if caring for a child.
Every gardener has enjoyed the time spent with a rose when
the rose is magnificently beautiful, but every gardener also
knows that the other side of a beautiful rose is one that fails
to flourish and requires much attention with little reward.
Overall, however, the benefits outweigh the disappointments,
and a gardener's whole life is affected by the fruits of his
labor and the joy found in seeing a new blossom burst into
existence.

I can't help thinking, however, that what we are seeing
is the "fallen" version of this species and that a rose in the
Garden of Eden would look different; it would be thornless,
disease free, always in flower and always fragrant, and would
require no maintenance!

What features in the current rose can be seen to represent
love—and what kind of love does it represent? While roman-
tic love is the first to come to mind, surely a more substantial
agape love is represented as well.

A list of features would start at the flower itself, noted for
its beauty, purity, softness, variety of shape and color, and of
course its fragrance. Then comes the abundance of petals, the
amount of blooms per bush, and just how impressive it is.

How we are attracted to the flower—as we are with love
itself—and nearly all of us have an impression left with us after
experiencing all these features. Everyone with whom some sort
of love is shared, received, or given leaves a lasting impression
on our lives.

A God who is described in Psalms as knowing all about us
even before we came into being and still was happy for that to
happen must be the ultimate rose!

There are some minor connected features of beauty in
this plant that should be noted as well, such as the shape of
the bush, the color of foliage, and the lovely orange hip that
appears in due course if allowed. Love comes in different
forms and strengths; it stays for fleeting moments or it lasts for
eternity.

The "fallen" side of this plant is most obviously found in
the thorns, which remind us that even the most beautifully
cultivated human version and character of love is flawed and
cannot be called perfect and without blemish; diseases and
pests love to attack and feed off the rosebush just as our enemy
and accuser cannot stand any form of love and tries to destroy
all forms of it in our lives. There is only one kind of perfect
love, found in and given by God—this kind of rose-love has
not a thorn or pest or disease.

Its beauty and fragrance are so strong as to be irresistible
to those who search for and find it or who stumble upon it
unplanned.

Lastly, our humble, flawed rose cannot produce its best
without constant maintenance and intervention. It is a prisoner
of season, it blesses us greatly for a time and starves us cruelly
for a while as well, but always, we in the garden are convinced
how bleak and impoverished our display is without it.

About the Photographer

MAL AUSTIN is one of Australia's most prominent Christian artists with a camera. A former schoolteacher, Mal now devotes his time to capturing the beauty of nature and crafting it into posters, gift cards, calendars, and books.

Eighteen years of commercial photography saw him complete over 650 weddings and hundreds of family portraits and advertising assignments. In 2000, Mal began a new photographic direction and vision under the name of Givenworks, believing God had given him new works to do. He specializes in the use of a panoramic film camera, and his work takes him deep into the Australian and New Zealand countryside to capture many isolated places with untouched landscapes.

Mal also works in close-up floral images with an emphasis on color, pattern, shape, and texture. While some images used in this book are from large-format Pentax and Bronica film cameras, most are digitally captured using Nikon D70 and D80 cameras.

www.givenworks.com

COLOR:
While bright is beautiful, God gave us subtle variations in all colors—each equally important. He has given us billions of recognizable colors for our enjoyment and use.

LIGHT:
Any subject suddenly comes alive when a sliver of morning light hits it. Jesus is our morning light, bringing us to life and changing us for the better.

CLOSE-UP:
God is a God of details. Look closely and you will see beauty in every feature. Don't be afraid to draw close to God. Beauty increases in closeness.

SHAPE:
Every rose and every leaf is unique by design and is then changed by weather and time, but our changes are best coming from God's Spirit.

TEXTURE:
Smooth, rough, sharp, scaly; textures create interest in nature. Let time, choices, and life's experience work to form beautiful patterns in us as well.

ENVIRONMENT:
God's environment provides dew, light, sun, food, and life cycles necessary for each plant to grow. He not only meets our needs but shapes our lives in extra dimensions.

BUGS:
The close-up beauty and color of hairy legs and glistening cobwebs; all in their place and for the purpose He intended.

AGING:
Plants have a life cycle, just as we do. Each stage brings beautiful new shapes and rich, powerful colors. God loves and values life in all its glorious stages.

IN SITU:
All the images in this book were taken in their natural place of growth. We, too, grow best in the place God has chosen for us.

Psalm 139

God Knows Me

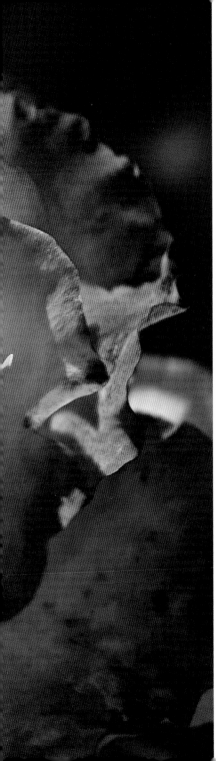

LORD, YOU HAVE EXAMINED ME
AND KNOW ALL ABOUT ME.
YOU KNOW WHEN I SIT DOWN
AND WHEN I GET UP.
YOU KNOW MY THOUGHTS
BEFORE I THINK THEM.

YOU KNOW
WHERE I GO
AND WHERE
I LIE DOWN.
YOU KNOW
THOROUGHLY
EVERYTHING
I DO.
LORD, EVEN
BEFORE I SAY
A WORD,
YOU ALREADY
KNOW IT.

You are all around me
- in front and in back -
and have put
your hand on me.

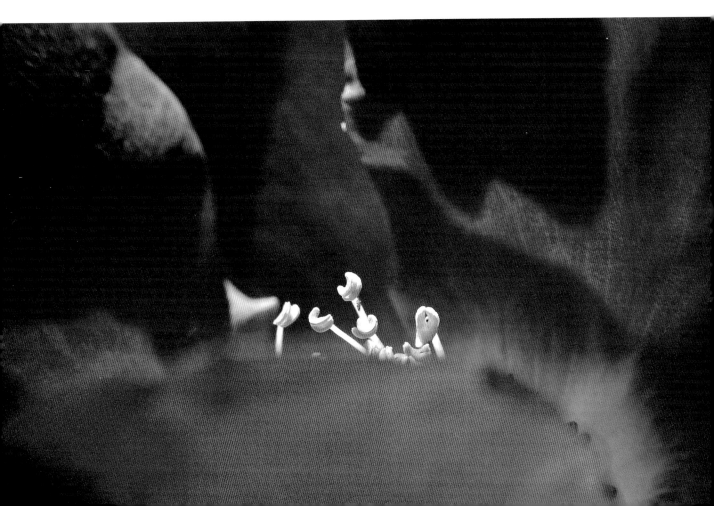

*Your knowledge
is amazing to me:
it is more
than I can understand.*

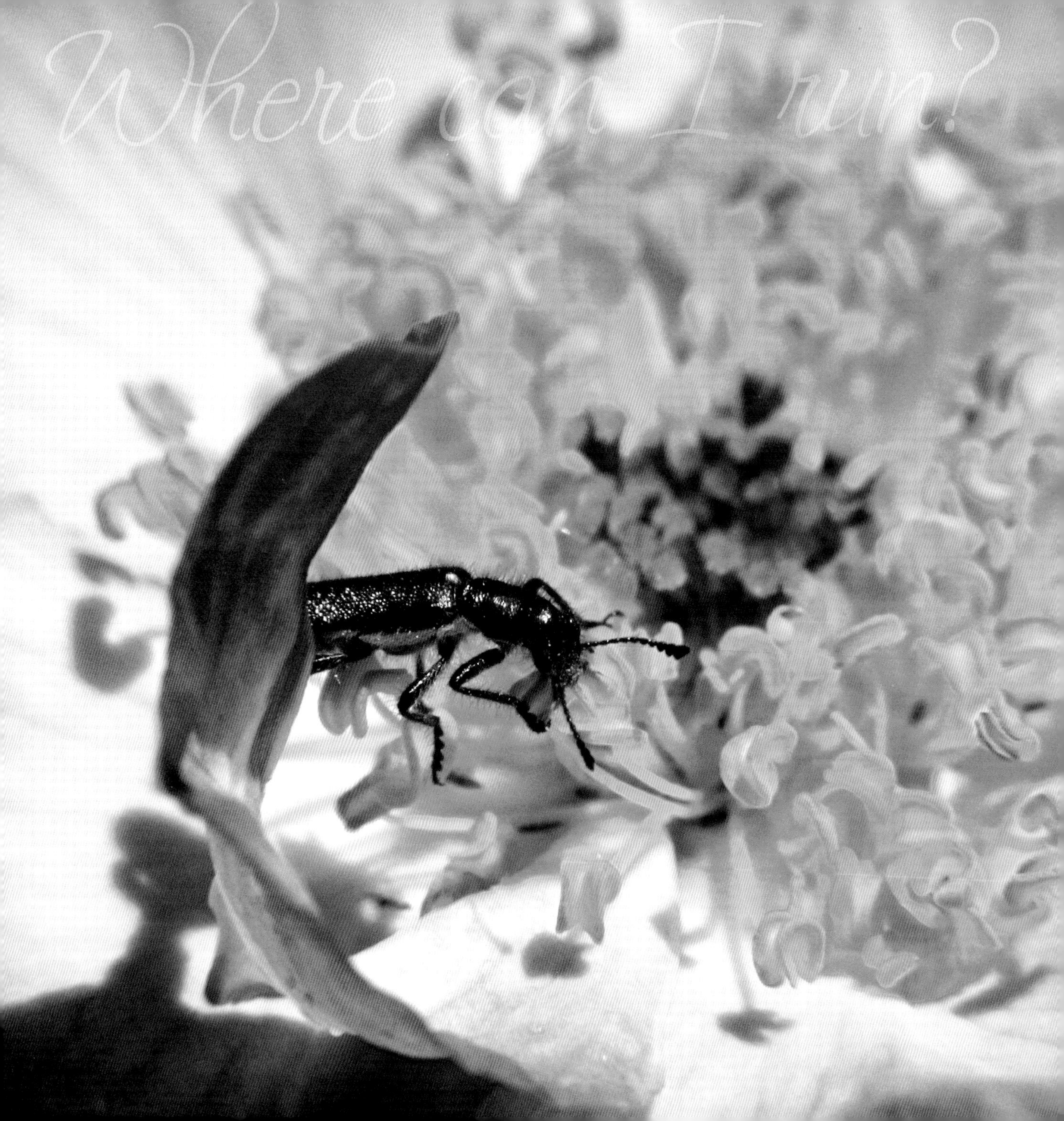
Where can I run?

Where can I go
to get away from your Spirit?
Where can I run from you?

IF I GO UP TO THE HEAVENS,
YOU ARE THERE.
IF I LIE DOWN IN THE
GRAVE, YOU ARE THERE.
IF I RISE WITH THE SUN
IN THE EAST AND
SETTLE IN THE WEST
BEYOND THE SEA,
EVEN THERE YOU
WOULD GUIDE ME.
WITH YOUR RIGHT HAND
YOU WOULD GUIDE ME.

I could say, "The darkness will hide me.
Let the light around me turn into night."

But even the darkness
is not dark to you.
The night is as light as the day;
darkness and light
are the same to you.

I am there for you

YOU MADE
MY WHOLE BEING:
YOU FORMED ME
IN MY MOTHER'S BODY.

I love you

I praise you
because you made me
in an amazing
and wonderful way.

You saw my bones being formed
as I took shape in my mother's body.
When I was put together there,
you saw my body as it was formed.

All the days planned for me
were written in your book
before I was one day old.

I think about you

I know you

GOD, YOUR THOUGHTS ARE PRECIOUS TO ME.

THEY ARE SO MANY!

IF I COULD COUNT THEM,

THEY WOULD BE MORE THAN ALL THE GRAINS OF SAND.

When I wake up, I am still with you.

God,
examine
me and
know
my heart:
test me
and
know my
nervous
thoughts.

everlasting

See if there is any
bad thing in me.
Lead me on the road
to everlasting life.

Psalm 121

God Protects Me

I look up to the hills,
but where does my help come from?
My help comes from the Lord,
who made heaven and earth.

help from the Lord

HE WILL NOT LET YOU BE DEFEATED.
HE WHO GUARDS YOU
NEVER SLEEPS.
HE WHO GUARDS ISRAEL
NEVER RESTS OR SLEEPS.

The Lord never sleeps

The Lord guards you.
The Lord is the shade
that protects you from the sun.

protection

The sun
cannot hurt
you during
the day,
and the moon
cannot hurt
you at night.

and safety

THE LORD WILL PROTECT YOU
FROM ALL DANGERS:
HE WILL GUARD YOUR LIFE.

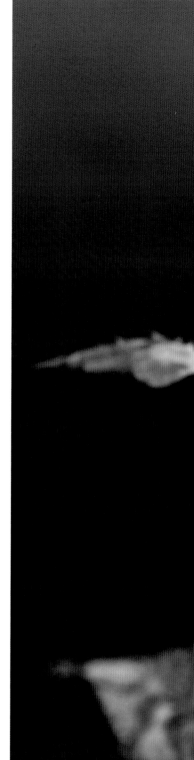

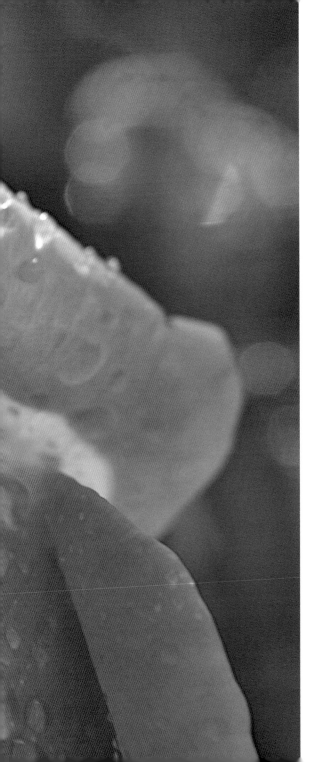

The Lord will guard you
as you come and go,
both now, and forever.

Our purpose at Howard Books is to:
• *Increase faith* in the hearts of growing Christians
• *Inspire holiness* in the lives of believers
• *Instill hope* in the hearts of struggling people everywhere
Because He's coming again!

Published by Howard Books, a Division of Simon & Schuster, Inc.
1230 Avenue of the Americas, New York, NY 10020
www.howardpublishing.com

Picture Psalms: A Season of Love © 2007 by Mal Austin

ISBN-13: 978-1-4165-5036-5
ISBN-10:   1-4165-5036-4
10 9 8 7 6 5 4 3 2 1

First Howard hardcover edition January 2008

HOWARD and colophon are registered trademarks of Simon & Schuster, Inc.

Manufactured in China

For information regarding special discounts for bulk purchases, please contact Simon & Schuster Special Sales at 1-800-456-6798 or business@simonandschuster.com.

Edited by Chrys Howard
Cover and interior design by Stephanie D. Walker

Scripture quotations taken from the *Holy Bible, New Century Version*. Copyright © 1987, 1988, 1991, by Thomas Nelson, Inc. Used by permission. All rights reserved.